My book for kids with cansur

by Jason Gaes

illustrated by Tim and Adam Gaes

MELIUS & PETERSON PUBLISHING INC.

Aberdeen, South Dakota

First Edition

Published in the United States by Melius & Peterson Publishing
Corporation, 524 Citizens Building, Aberdeen, South Dakota
57401.

Illustrations: Adam and Tim Gaes
Book and Cover Design: Victoria Cavalier

Third Printing

Library of Congress Cataloging-in-Publication Data

Gaes, Jason, 1977–
    My book for kids with cansur [sic]

    Summary: A young boy describes his successful two-year
battle with cancer and offers advice to other cancer
patients.
    1. Gaes, Jason, 1977–   --Health--Juvenile literature.
2. Tumors in children--Patients--United States--Biography--
Juvenile literature. [1. Gaes, Jason, 1977–
2. Cancer--Patients. 3. Children's writings] I. Gaes,
Adam, ill. II. Gaes, Tim, ill. III. Title.
RC281.C4G34 1987   616.99'4'00924 [B] [92]   87-60794
ISBN 0-937603-04-X

Sister Margaret

I dedicate this book to Margaret cause we're both waiting to see if our cansur comes back.

My name is Jason Gaes. I live at 1109 Omaha ave. in Worthington, Mn. I am 8 yrs. old and I have cansur.

My cansur started when I was 6 yrs. old and I was at my Gramma Gaes house. My uncl Terry looked in my mouth with a flashlight and saw a bump by one of my teeth. The dr. said he had to have a pees of the bump to see what was inside. There was cansur inside. Then the drs in Rochester found lots of more bumps inside of me. There called toomers.

The first toomer was inside of my head behind my eye. Thats why I had crossed eyes. I had radiashun on my head and that bump melted. So now my eyes arent crossed anymore. Radiashun was really eezee. All you have to do is lay there and they put straps around your head so you don't moov and then it's over and you come back toomarow. But don't wash the X's off your head until there done.

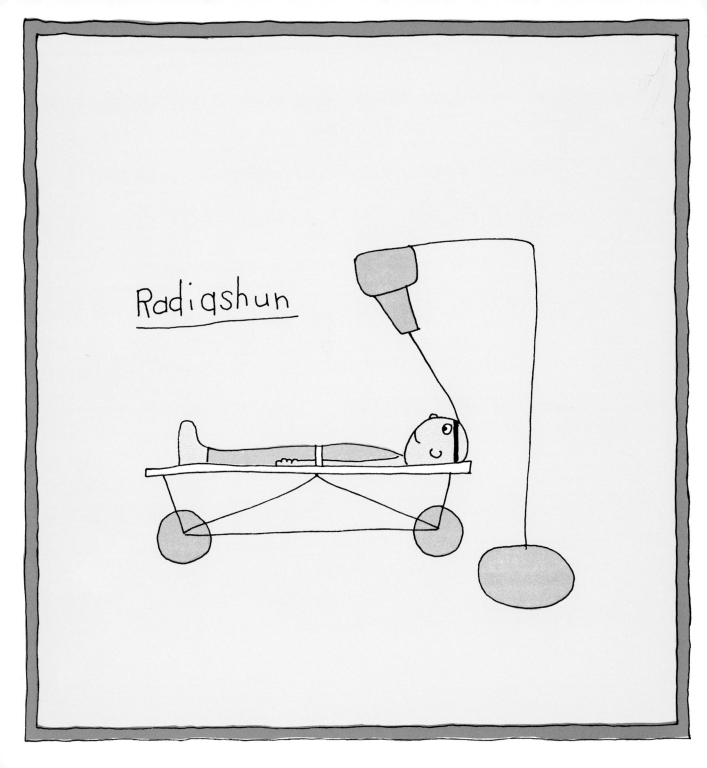

The next toomer was in my stumick.
I could feel that one when I
layed down so they operated that
one out Operating toomers out is
alot harder than radiashun them
out but your a sleep so you don't
need to be scared.

Hospitals are fun about the first 2 or 3 days. Then they get boring so bring coloring books and toys for when cartoons aren't on. If you're grown up bring cards.

Then I had toomers on the kidnees
so I take medasin that melts those.
It's called keymotharupy. Keymotharupy
is medasin that drips out of a needl
in your arm called a IV or a shot
in your back called a spinal.

Ivs

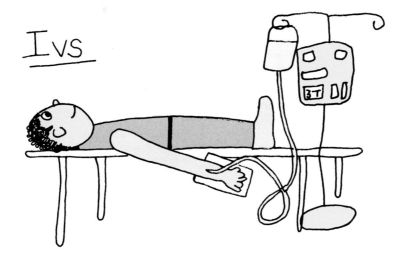

Sometimes keymotharupy makes you sick and you throw up. Sometimes you looz your hair from it but you can wear hats if it bothers you. Mostly kids don't care when your bald. And if they laff or make fun there not very good friends anyway. Some kids think its cool.

The rezin I wanted to write a book about having cansur is because every book I read about kids with cansur they alwdys die. I want to tell you kids dont always die. If you get cansur dont be scared cause lots of people get over having cansur and grow up without dying. Like Mike Nelson and Doug Cerny and Vince Varpness and President Reagan and me.

Having cansur isnt fun. In fact its the pits but its not all bad either. You get lots of cards and presents when your in the hospital. You have to have cansur to get in vited to go to Camp Courage.

When your bald you dont have to worry about getting shampoo in your eyes when your sick from a treetment you get to stay home from school and when your done having cansur you get to have a big party. The best party in your whole life.

My Party

There are a couple bad parts of having cansur too. There's blood tests. I got used to those so I could go in by myself but if your scared of blood tests have your mom or Dad cover your eyes. If you cant see the needle it doesn't hurt as much as if your sister pinches you. And you don't cry everytime you get pinched do you?

Then there's putting an iv in
your hand and spinals and bone
mairos. Ivs aren't so bad.
The nurses say done before
you get to 3. The spinals and
bone mairos are bad no matter
how far you count but they go
faster if you curl up tight and try
to relacks. That's hard to do
but try thinking about your party
till the bad part is over.

Being scared is a bad part of cansur too. It makes you feel bad and makes your stumick hurt. But Dr Karen will tell you what is going to hurt so you dont need to be afraid of everything. And it doesnt help to be afraid anyway. If you get cansur you might as well not even be afraid cause your probly not even going to die anyway.

Waking up at night scared.

If you can find it get a poster that says Help me to remember Lord that nothing is gonna happen today that you and me can't handle together. Then hang it in your room and redd it at night when your scared. If you get scared and cant quit go and talk to your Mom and she can rock you or rub your hair.

Or if you want you can call me. My number is 507 376-3824. and when you feel real bad its ok to cry Sometimes. It doesn't mean your a baby and Dr. Karen says sometimes it makes you feel better.
Is Jason there?

And the rest of the days when you don't have a treetment try to forget you have cansyr and think about something else. Shoot baskets or go swimming.

Sometimes even if you do everything just like everybody else a pees of your cansur can break off and go to your lungs and grow there. If the drs cant get it out then your probly gonna die when your a kid. My Mom said when me and Tim was babys in her stumick we liked it in there so good the dr had to give my Mom a shot to make us come out. But now that I'm outside I wouldnt never want to go back.

She says going to heaven is probly like that. Once we get there we won't want to come back here. We'r just scared about going to heaven because we never been there. You can see your Grandpa again and pretty soon your Mom will be there too. Then Adam or Tim cause every bodys godda die sometime.

Sometimes when your sick from a treetment you miss school but try to make up your work cause colij makes you have all your work done before you can be a doctor. And I'm going to be a doctor who takes care of kids with cansur so I can tell them what its like.